GALILEE

Capernaum

Cana

Lake of Tiberias

Nazareth

DECAPOLIS

MEDITERRANEAN

60 miles

SAMARIA

PEREA

JUDEA

Jerusalem

Ain Karim

Bethlehem

to Egypt

Dead Sea

JESUS IN HIS EARLY YEARS

This album describes only those passages where the Bible indicates that Mary is present and one or two others where she might well have been. Some episodes (notably the crucifixion) are seen briefly through her eyes and are treated at greater length in other volumes.

Editorial Committee
Father René Berthier

Jeanne-Marie Faure

Marie-Hélène Sigaut

Illustrated by
Régine and Bruno Le Sourd

British Library Cataloguing in Publication Data
Berthier, René
    1. Jesus Christ — Childhood — Juvenile literature
    I. Jesus in his early years
232.9'2   BT320

ISBN 0 340 24054 7

First published 1979

Printed in Belgium for Hodder & Stoughton Ltd.,
Mill Road, Dunton Green, Sevenoaks, Kent, by
Henri Proost & Cie, Turnhout.

HODDER AND STOUGHTON
LONDON SYDNEY AUCKLAND TORONTO

SOMEWHERE
ALONG THE SHORES
OF THE MEDITERRANEAN,
40 TO 50 YEARS
AFTER THE DEATH OF JESUS.

Listen, Luke: a lot of things have been written about Jesus, but they need to be put into some kind of order. You have a real talent for writing, so why don't you do it?

Learn as much as you can, and then put it clearly in writing.

Mark has already done that and you know what a big help that has been to us.

you could read his account and add what the Lord taught us around here.

Now that we know he is the Saviour, we understand better what he did and what he taught.

They're right. They have seen and heard Jesus when he was alive, and they know the truth about him.

MATTHEW'S GOSPEL WAS WRITTEN ABOUT THE SAME TIME. JOHN COMPLETED HIS GOSPEL SOME 10 OR 15 YEARS LATER. SO, THANKS TO THE FOUR EVANGELISTS AND THE SPIRIT OF GOD WORKING WITH THEM, WE ARE ABLE, ALMOST 2000 YEARS LATER, TO KNOW JESUS, THE SON OF GOD AND SON OF MARY.

I am the servant of the Lord. Let him make use of me in whatever way he wants.

MARY!

What is it, Mary? Are you sick?

Don't worry. Everything's all right.

I must go away for a while. Our cousin Elizabeth is going to have a baby.

What! Elizabeth? She's much too old! And she's never been able to have a child.

It's a sign from God. Her child will be a great man.

How did you find that out?

A messenger from god has just told me.

?

What about Joseph?

Do me a favour. Tell him I'm going away for a while.

How radiant she looks! I'm sure she hasn't told me everything

THAT NIGHT . . .

But it's my son I'm thinking of. Will he be dressed like a king? For I clearly heard: "He will be king of our people for ever." What does it mean? Will he be like King David?

Do you like my cloth?

Yes, it is pretty.

Please! would you hold him for a moment?

I'd love to!

Mine will be great. He will be holy. He will be called the son of the Most High. It's all so wonderful! Am I dreaming it?

MOST BLESSED ARE YOU AMONG ALL WOMEN!
AND BLESSED, TOO, IS YOUR SON!

WHAT AN HONOUR FOR ME!
THE MOTHER OF MY LORD HAS COME TO ME!

AND WHAT A GREAT JOY FOR YOU:
YOU HAVE BELIEVED IN THE WORD OF THE
LORD.

I REJOICE IN THE GLORY OF THE LORD,
MY HEART IS FILLED WITH JOY!

I HAVE SO LITTLE TO OFFER
AND YET MY SAVIOUR HAS LOOKED FAVOURABLY
UPON ME.

YES, THE WHOLE WORLD WILL HONOUR ME:
HOW HAPPY I AM!

THE LORD HAS DONE GREAT THINGS FOR ME.
HE IS STRONG AND HOLY.
HE LOVES EVERYONE!

AS HIS OWN POWER UNFOLDS
EARTH'S POWERFUL ONES ARE THROWN DOWN
AND THE LITTLE ONES ARE RAISED ON HIGH.

THOSE WHO ARE HUNGRY WILL HAVE PLENTY TO EAT.
AND THE RICH WILL BE LEFT WITHOUT ANYTHING.

OH YES, PRAISE THE LORD
WHO IS FAITHFUL TO HIS PEOPLE
AND TENDERLY WATCHES OVER ALL OF US.

ALL THIS TIME JOSEPH HAS REMAINED AT HOME.

Doesn't it bother you?

Is your wedding postponed?

It's certainly strange that your fiancee went away so suddenly!

And for three months...

Oh, be quiet, you're driving me mad!

Hello, there!

This is broken. Can you fix it?

Let me see.

Phew! What a trip! I've come all the way beyond Jerusalem.

What's the news from around there?

Still Romans Romans all over the place!

Let's drink a toast to their defeat!

Ssh! Someone might hear us.

There was a story going around about a very extraordinary event in one of the nearby villages.

What?

A priest's barren wife had a baby.

Any more?

The story goes that the father had a vision, and then he couldn't speak until the day his son was born.

Who are the parents?

Zechariah and Elizabeth, I think.

Mary was there. Perhaps she'd guessed something was in the air.

SOME TIME LATER, AT MARY'S HOME.

Hello, Mary. I'd heard that you'd come back.

Hello, Joseph. I'm so glad to see you.

Are you all right? You look tired.

The journey...

14

MONTHS LATER

Hear ye: The Emperor Caesar Augustus, reigning from Rome, has decreed that a census be taken of the population of the Empire. By his command every family must register at the place that it came from.

Another crazy Roman idea.

Another way to pester us.

That's going to be hard for us—the baby so close to birth.

We have no choice. We have to go...

THEY SET OUT FOR BETHLEHEM, A LONG WAY AWAY

Keep going Mary, we're almost there.

Where are you from?

Damascus. And you?

Alexandria in Egypt.

You belong to the family of King David?

Then, we're cousins!

Would you let us go ahead of you, please? My wife is exhausted.

Of course. She looks as if her baby's about ready to arrive. I know from my own experience.

Your names, address, occupation...

What a crowd! Where will we ever find lodging?

No vacancy here! No room for you.

We must find somewhere at once. There's no time!

Maybe we'll find a quiet spot. Over there!

We must hurry, Joseph. I feel I'm due now.

Here. This may not be too bad.

15

DAYS PASSED ...

THAT NIGHT, AT AN INN.

How horrible!

It was Herod who ordered this slaughter

To think that monster is our king!

Sh... not so loud.

Who's he after?

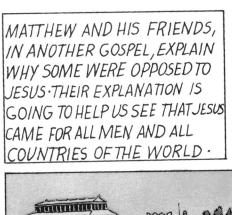

MATTHEW AND HIS FRIENDS, IN ANOTHER GOSPEL, EXPLAIN WHY SOME WERE OPPOSED TO JESUS. THEIR EXPLANATION IS GOING TO HELP US SEE THAT JESUS CAME FOR ALL MEN AND ALL COUNTRIES OF THE WORLD.

HEROD'S PALACE IN JERUSALEM

Who are these people who are spreading these stories? They're going to cause trouble.

They are astrologers, wise men who interpret the stars. They've been here for several days.

They've come from far away. They're foreigners.

They're looking for a certain newborn child.

This could be serious.

They'd believe anything from a horoscope.

All the same, there's some truth in them sometimes.

Gentlemen, what have you found out?

We suggest that experts in religion and in the Bible would be able to give you some useful information about this so-called king.

Good! Send in these experts.

Here are the chief priests, and these are the scribes.

Do you know where the Messiah is to be born? What do the scriptures say about it?

At Bethlehem in Judaea.

Good! I thank you. You may leave.

You! Stay here!

Listen: bring these wise men here at once. And keep this a secret: no one is to know about this.

I'll set off at once.

SOON AFTERWARDS ···

From our detailed observations, found by study of the heavenly constellations, we have concluded that...

Skip all that. What have you found out?

At this moment a new light is rising which will light up the whole world.

This is, I believe what your prophets announce in your holy books.

From that, we conclude that a "star" is now rising over the Jewish people.

And the whole world will look to this marvellous child of your people.

Your thinking is flawless. There is only one thing to do.

We want to be the first to honour him.

How long is it since this "light" appeared?

A short time. A few months, maybe.

Do you know exactly where this little "wonder" lives?

No, we haven't found out yet. We would like to appeal to your great kindness to help us.

Go to Bethlehem. You'll very likely find some help there.

And, listen, bring back news to me as quickly as possible. This is of very great interest to me.

We are very grateful to your Majesty.

We're certainly lucky to get this information.

If a person is sincere, he usually succeeds in whatever he does.

Yes, but I don't trust that Herod. We must be very careful.

Wait here for us.

We'd better not mention anything about a "king". We'll inquire only about a small child.

Go, Moses. I am sending you to lead my people out of Egypt.

Who will be sent so that all men will be completely free?

Funny little fellow! Where do you dig up all these ideas?

When Israel was delivered from oppression, the sea parted and the earth showed its joy.

Alleluia! Alleluia!

Alleluia!

Alleluia!

Why do we celebrate the Passover by eating roast lamb?

To remind us of what the Almighty has done. Our forefathers ate lamb in earlier times as they were about to escape from slavery.

Honour to our God! Bless his name!

WHEN THE FEAST WAS ENDED THE JOURNEY HOME BEGAN.

Where is Jesus? Why hasn't he joined us?

Is Jesus with you?

No, we don't know where he is. We haven't seen him all day.

Jesus? No, I haven't seen him.

No, I'm afraid not.

I'm worried. I've looked among the pilgrims but no one has seen him. He never has been disobedient.

It's just not like him to do such a thing.

Something must have happened to him. Maybe it happened in Jerusalem.

We must go back, right away.

No, we haven't seen him.

We've searched the porticos, the courtyards, the streets all around. Still no luck.

We should have watched him more closely.

Don't worry yourself. Let's try to get some rest. We'll look for him again tomorrow.

This is the only place left.

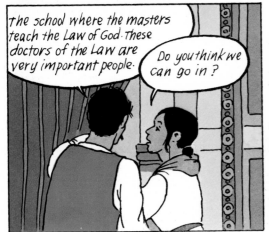

The school where the masters teach the Law of God. These doctors of the Law are very important people.

Do you think we can go in?

Tell me, how is God going to deliver our people today?

The teachers are going to have a hard time to answer him. His questions are difficult.

This child is extremely intelligent.

He thinks beyond his years. He seems to understand instinctively the things of God.

JESUS RETURNED TO NAZARETH WITH THEM, AND REMAINED THERE FOR ALMOST TWENTY YEARS, LIVING THE UNEVENTFUL LIFE OF A CARPENTER IN A GALILEAN VILLAGE.

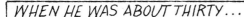

Mother, as you know, John is preaching at the River Jordan. I am going there to join him.

When will you be back?

I don't know. I won't be using the workshop any more. There are other things I must do now.

I knew this day would come; my heart will go with you, Jesus.

Look, there are our sons.

James, Mark, did you have a good trip? Are you satisfied with what you got?

Oh yes, our sacks are full. Dried fish, some salt, some tools...

We have some for everyone.

What's new in Capernaum?

There's a lot going on. And we met Jesus. Did you know that he's preaching now.

Your son, Jesus?

He's a good preacher. We've heard him. Everyone's drawn to him.

That's his true work. Now I realize that.

Jesus? Surely not! A prophet is quite different... John the Baptist lives in the desert, never drinks wine. But Jesus... why, he always been just like the rest of us.

Anyway, he's already made very many friends.

He's living with one of them — a fellow called Simon, a fisherman by trade.

I'm curious to hear him.

Me, too.

JOHN'S GOSPEL PORTRAYS JESUS AS ONE WHO BRINGS JOY AND ABUNDANCE WITH HIM. THAT IS WHY HE PRESENTS THE WEDDING AT CANA AS A SIGN OF JOYOUS RENEWAL.

Mary, are you coming to the wedding? And would you tell Jesus we'd love to have him with us. His friends are welcome as well.

Thank you. I'll tell him about your invitation.

Jesus, we're so glad you've come.

John, Simon, come on in.

30

IN GALILEE, WALKING FROM VILLAGE TO VILLAGE, JESUS MEETS PEOPLE, HEALS THEM AND SHOWS THEM HOW MUCH GOD CARES FOR THEM.

AT NAZARETH HE AMAZES PEOPLE.

AT MAGDALA

I have good news for you: the kingdom of God is very near. Believe me.

What a dreamer! With all this misery in the world... what's going to change that!

I have a feeling that through Jesus it's already beginning to change. Look how he inspires new hope in people's hearts

that one! She needs to weep for her sins! She's got plenty of them on her conscience.

Mary of Magdala... who knows? Maybe she's discovering something...

AT BETHSAIDA

The kingdom of God is very near, now. Believe me! Change your attitudes and your ways.

IN THE COURSE OF HIS TRAVELS HE RETURNS TO NAZARETH...

Jesus is here!

Let's go and hear him!

Let's go: to the house of prayer!

Everyone— to the synagogue!

Would anyone like to read for us?

Would you read from the book of the prophet Isaiah!

The spirit of God is upon me. I belong entirely to him. He has sent me to bring the Good News to the poor, to proclaim liberation to the imprisoned, to give sight to the blind, to set the oppressed free, to announce the good deeds of God.

They say he speaks very well. I wonder...

We'll soon find out.

This passage from the book of Isaiah has come true, here, today, before your eyes.

?

That text Jesus read is all about the Messiah.

Precisely.

Then, does that mean Jesus regards himself as the Messiah?

Impossible! Jesus has always lived here among us.

He's just a carpenter—and that's all there is to it!

We know his mother very well. Here she is now.

34

It's a nuisance Jesus isn't here. I had some work for him to do.

He won't be back too soon. You know what's being said? He's drawing such crowds that he and his friends can hardly find time to eat!

But he's going to make enemies for himself by the way he's criticizing the religious leaders.

He's mad! He's completely out of his mind!

NO! He knows what he's doing... ...but how is it all going to end?

He'd be better to come back here and settle down quietly and peacefully.

We must bring him to his senses. Let's go and find him.

Come with us, Mary. Maybe all of us together can persuade him.

Yes. This news distresses me. I'm coming with you.

Who is my mother? Who are my brothers?

Whoever does God's will— they are my brothers, my sisters, my mother.

I should have known Jesus is completely caught up in God's work. O Lord, protect him in your love.

SOME TIME LATER, JESUS RETURNS HOME TO NAZARETH.

Jesus will be here in a little while.

About time too! We've scarcely seen him in months.

That's not surprising. We don't run after him the way they do in other places. We know him too well to do that.

It's the same with his healing. He does hardly any around here.

You want special favours just because you belong to the same family and country as he does. But you refuse to believe in him.

You're his mother. Of course you'll take sides with him, that's to be expected. But I can't get over the way he treated us in Capernaum.

His relatives and his mother have confidence in him.

O.K., let's go hear this prophet-son of yours!

I bet you're going to quote this proverb to me: "Doctor, heal yourself," and ask me to do here what I did in Capernaum.

I tell you the truth: no prophet is well received in his own country.

He's needling us!

Who does he think he is, anyway!

37

Remember what the prophets did:

ELIJAH; during the great famine, there were many widows in Israel. Nevertheless, whom did he help? The widow of Zarephath, a complete stranger!

And the prophet ELISHA: there were many lepers in Israel then. And yet, he went and cured a leper from Syria, a foreign land.

He's gone too far!

He's not going to get away with that!

We'll smash his face! He's asking for trouble.

Not here! outside.

Get him out of town.

What's happening?

We're fed up with him. He's no longer one of us.

He's mad and dangerous.

I don't believe it!

Down, you...!

We'll soon see if he's going to keep on insulting us.

BUT JESUS PASSED THROUGH THE CROWD AND WENT ON HIS WAY.

38

They just don't understand that he wants the best for them. Thank you God for being with him. Please protect him.

I can't stay here any longer. I want to be with him — to share his joys, his dangers.

Goodbye, Nazareth

JESUS LEAVES NAZARETH, AND GOES SOUTHWARD INTO JUDEA,
AND MARY SHARES HIS SORROWS AND HIS JOYS.
JESUS COMES INTO CONFLICT WITH ALL THOSE WHOSE HEARTS ARE HARDENED.
THE RELIGIOUS LEADERS IN JERUSALEM DECIDE TO PUT HIM TO DEATH.

ONE FRIDAY MORNING

It's James, John's brother. Open up.

They arrested him last night.

We were afraid something awful would happen.

Have you the courage to go, Mary? Aren't you afraid?

It doesn't matter what happens to me. I want to be with him to the very end.

We're going with you!

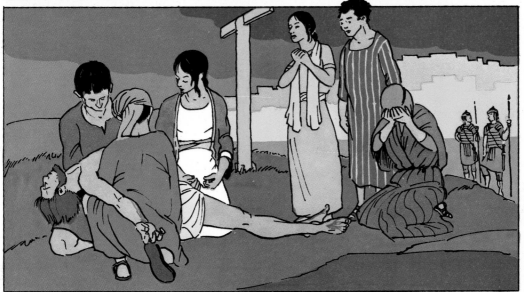

40

GIVE THANKS TO THE LORD, FOR HE IS GOOD.
HE HAS SAVED HIS MESSIAH FROM DEATH.
HIS LOVE ENDURES FOR EVER.
HE HAS OPENED THE GATES OF LIFE.
YES, HIS LOVE EXTENDS FOR EVER.

Passages from the Gospels

which have inspired this book

The text is taken from the NEW INTERNATIONAL VERSION of the Bible.
Page numbers refer to this volume.

Luke 1:1-4   page 3
Many have undertaken to draw up an account of the things that have been fulfilled among us, **2** just as they were handed down to us by those who from the first were eye-witnesses and servants of the word. **3** Therefore, since I myself have carefully investigated everything from the beginning, it seemed good also to me to write an orderly account for you, most excellent Theophilus, **4** so that you may know the certainty of the things you have been taught.

The visit of the angel

Luke 1:26-38   pages 4-6
26 In the sixth month, God sent the angel Gabriel to Nazareth, a town in Galilee, **27** to a virgin pledged to be married to a man named Joseph, a descendant of David. The virgin's name was Mary. **28** The angel went to her and said, "Greetings, you who are highly favoured! The Lord is with you."

29 Mary was greatly troubled at his words and wondered what kind of greeting this might be. **30** But the angel said to her, "Do not be afraid, Mary, you have found favour with God. **31** You will be with child and give birth to a son, and you are to give him the name Jesus. **32** He will be great and will be called the Son of the Most High. The Lord God will give him the throne of his father David, **33** and he will reign over the house of Jacob for ever; his kingdom will never end."

34 "How can this be," Mary asked the angel, "since I am a virgin?"

35 The angel answered, "The Holy Spirit will come upon you, and the power of the Most High will overshadow you. So the holy one to be born will be called the Son of God. **36** Even Elizabeth your relative is going to have a child in her old age, and she who was said to be barren is in her sixth month. **37** For nothing is impossible with God."

38 "I am the Lord's servant," Mary answered. "May it be to me as you have said." Then the angel left her.

Mary and Elizabeth

Luke 1:39-56   pages 7-11
39 At that time Mary got ready and hurried to a town in the hill country of Judah, **40** where she entered Zechariah's home and greeted Elizabeth. **41** When Elizabeth heard Mary's greeting, the baby leaped in her womb, and Elizabeth was filled with the Holy Spirit. **42** In a loud voice she exclaimed: "Blessed are you among women and blessed is the child you will bear! **43** But why am I so favoured, that the mother of my Lord should come to me? **44** As soon as the sound of your greeting reached my ears, the baby in my womb leaped for joy. **45** Blessed is she who has believed that what the Lord has said to her will be accomplished!"

46 And Mary said:
"My soul praises the Lord
47 and my spirit rejoices in God my Saviour,
48 for he has been mindful of the humble state of his servant.
From now on all generations will call me blessed,
49 for the Mighty One has done great things for me — holy is his name.

50 His mercy extends to those who fear him, from generation to generation.

51 He has performed mighty deeds with his arm; he has scattered those who are proud in their inmost thoughts.

52 He has brought down rulers from their thrones but has lifted up the humble.

53 He has filled the hungry with good things but has sent the rich away empty.

54 He has helped his servant Israel, remembering to be merciful

55 to Abraham and his descendants for ever, even as he said to our fathers."

56 Mary stayed with Elizabeth for about three months and then returned home.

The birth of John

Luke 1:57-80　　　　　　　　　　　　　　　page 12

57 When it was time for Elizabeth to have her baby, she gave birth to a son. 58 Her neighbours and relatives heard that the Lord had shown her great mercy, and they shared her joy.

59 On the eighth day they came to circumcise the child, and they were going to name him after his father Zechariah, 60 but his mother spoke up and said, "No! He is to be called John."

61 They said to her, "There is no one among your relatives who has that name."

62 Then they made signs to his father, to find out what he would like to name the child. 63 He asked for a writing tablet, and to everyone's astonishment he wrote, "His name is John." 64 Immediately his mouth was opened and his tongue was loosed, and he began to speak, praising God. 65 The neighbours were all filled with awe, and throughout the hill country of Judea people were talking about all these things. 66 Everyone who heard this wondered about it, asking, "What then is this child going to be?" For the Lord's hand was with him.

67 His father Zechariah was filled with the Holy Spirit and prophesied:

68 "Praise the Lord, the God of Israel, because he has come and redeemed his people.

69 He has raised up a horn of salvation for us in the house of his servant David

70 (as he said through his holy prophets of long ago),

71 salvation from our enemies
      and from the hand
         of all who hate us –

72 to show mercy to our fathers
      and to remember
         his holy convenant,

73 the oath he swore to our father Abraham:

74 to rescue us from the hand of our enemies, and to enable us to serve him without fear

75 in holiness and righteousness before him all our days.

76 And you, my child, will be called a prophet of the
         Most High;
      for you will go on before the Lord to
         prepare the way for him,

77 to give his people the knowledge of salvation
      through the forgiveness of their sins,

78 because of the tender mercy of our God,
      by which the rising sun will come to us from
         heaven

79 to shine on those living in darkness
      and in the shadow of death,
   to guide our feet into the path of peace."

80 And the child grew and became strong in spirit; and he lived in the desert until he appeared publicly to Israel.

Joseph's story

Matthew 1:18-25　　　　　　　　　　　　　page 14

18 This is how the birth of Jesus Christ came about. His mother Mary was pledged to be married to Joseph, but before they came together, she was found to be with child through the Holy Spirit. 19 Because Joseph her husband was a righteous man and did not want to expose her to public disgrace, he had in mind to divorce her quietly.

20 But after he had considered this, an angel of the Lord appeared to him in a dream and said, "Joseph son of David, do not be afraid to take Mary home as your wife, because what is conceived in her is from the Holy Spirit. 21 She will give birth to a son, and you are to give him the name Jesus, because he will save his people from their sins."

22 All this took place to fulfil what the Lord had said through the prophet: 23 "The virgin will be with child and will give birth to a son, and they will call him Immanuel" – which means, "God with us."

24 When Joseph woke up, he did what the angel of the Lord had commanded him and took Mary home as his wife. 25 But he had no union with her until she gave birth to a son. And he gave him the name Jesus.

The birth of Jesus

Luke 2:1-7　　　　　　　　　　　　　　　page 15

1 In those days Caesar Augustus issued a decree that a census should be taken of the entire Roman world. 2 (This was the first census that took place while Quirinius was governor of Syria.) 3 And everyone went to his own town to register.

4 So Joseph also went up from the town of Nazareth in Galilee to Judea, to Bethlehem the town of David, because he belonged to the house and line of David. 5 He went there to register with Mary, who was pledged to be married to him and was expecting a child. 6 While they were there, the time came for the baby to be born, 7 and she gave birth to her firstborn, a son. She wrapped him in strips of cloth and placed him in a manger, because there was no room for them in the inn.

The shepherds are told

Luke 2:8-20　　　　　　　　　　　　　　pages 16-17

8 And there were shepherds living out in the fields near by, keeping watch over their flocks at night. 9 An angel of the Lord appeared to them, and the glory of the Lord shone around them, and they were terrified. 10 But the angel said to them, "Do not be afraid. I bring you good news of great joy that will be for all people. 11 Today in the town of David a Saviour has been born to you; he is Christ the Lord. 12 This will be a sign to you: You will find a baby wrapped in strips of cloth and lying in a manger."

13 Suddenly a great company of the heavenly host appeared with the angel, praising God and saying, 14 "Glory to God in the highest, and on earth peace to men on whom his favour rests."

15 When the angels had left them and gone into heaven, the shepherds said to one another, "Let's go to Bethlehem and see this thing that has happened, which the Lord has told us about."

16 So they hurried off and found Mary and Joseph, and the baby, who was lying in the manger. 17 When they had seen him, they spread the word concerning what had been told them about this child, 18 and all who heard it were amazed at what the shepherds said to them. 19 But Mary treasured up all these things and pondered them in her mind. 20 The shepherds returned, glorifying and praising God for all the things they had heard and seen, which were just as they had been told.

The circumcision of Jesus

Luke 2:21   page 18

21 On the eighth day, when it was time to circumcise him, he was named Jesus, the name the angel had given him before he had been conceived.

Jesus is presented at the temple

Luke 2:22-40   page 19

22 When the time of their purification according to the Law of Moses had been completed, Joseph and Mary took him to Jerusalem to present him to the Lord 23 (as it is written in the Law of the Lord, "Every firstborn male is to be consecrated to the Lord"), 24 and to offer a sacrifice in keeping with what is said in the Law of the Lord: "A pair of doves or two young pigeons."

25 Now there was a man in Jerusalem called Simeon, who was righteous and devout. He was waiting for the consolation of Israel, and the Holy Spirit was upon him. 26 It had been revealed to him by the Holy Spirit that he would not die before he had seen the Lord's Christ. 27 Moved by the Spirit, he went into the temple courts. When the parents brought in the child Jesus to do for him as the custom of the Law required, 28 Simeon took him in his arms and praised God, saying:
29 "Sovereign Lord, as you promised,
    now dismiss your servant in peace.
30 For my eyes have seen your salvation,
    31 which you have prepared in the sight of all people,
32 a light for revelation to the Gentiles
    and for glory to your people Israel."
33 The child's father and mother marvelled at what was said about him. 34 Then Simeon blessed them and said to Mary, his mother: "This child is destined to cause the falling and rising of many in Israel, and to be a sign that will be spoken against, 35 so that the thoughts of many hearts will be revealed. And a sword will pierce your own soul too."

36 There was also a prophetess, Anna, the daughter of Phanuel, of the tribe of Asher. She was very old; she had lived with her husband seven years after her marriage, 37 and then was a widow until she was eighty-four. She never left the temple but worshiped night and day, fasting and praying. 38 Coming up to them at that very moment, she gave thanks to God and spoke about the child to all who were looking forward to the redemption of Jerusalem.

39 When Joseph and Mary had done everything required by the Law of the Lord, they returned to Galilee to their own town of Nazareth. 40 And the child grew and became strong; he was filled with wisdom, and the grace of God was upon him.

The men from the east

Matthew 2:1-12   pages 22-24

1 After Jesus was born in Bethlehem in Judea, during the time of King Herod, Magi from the east came to Jerusalem 2 and asked, "Where is the one who has been born king of the Jews? We saw his star in the east and have come to worship him."

3 When King Herod heard this he was disturbed, and all Jerusalem with him. 4 When he had called together all the chief priests and teachers of the law, he asked them where the Christ was to be born. 5 "In Bethlehem in Judea," they replied, "for this is what the prophet has written:
6 'And you, Bethlehem, in the land of Judah,
    are by no means least among the rulers of Judah;
for out of you will come a ruler
    who will be the shepherd of my people Israel.' "
7 Then Herod called the Magi secretly and found out from them the exact time the star had appeared. 8 He sent them to Bethlehem and said, "Go and make a careful search for the child. As soon as you find him, report to me, so that I too may go and worship him."

9 After they had heard the king, they went on their way, and the star they had seen in the east went ahead of them until it stopped over the place where the child was. 10 When they saw the star, they were overjoyed. 11 On coming to the house, they saw the child with his mother Mary, and they bowed down and worshipped him. Then they opened their treasures and presented him with gifts of gold and of incense and of myrrh. 12 And having been warned in a dream not to go back to Herod, they returned to their country by another route.

Joseph is warned

Matthew 2:13-15   page 20

13 When they had gone, an angel of the Lord appeared to Joseph in a dream. "Get up," he said, "take the child and his mother and escape to Egypt. Stay there until I tell you, for Herod is going to search for the child and kill him."

14 So he got up, took the child and his mother during the night and left for Egypt, 15 where he stayed until the death of Herod. And so was fulfilled what the Lord had said through the prophet: "I called my son out of Egypt."

The massacre of children

Matthew 2:16-18   page 21

16 When Herod realized that he had been outwitted by the Magi, he was furious, and he gave orders to kill all the boys in Bethlehem and its vicinity who were two years old and under, in accordance with the time he had learned from the Magi. 17 Then what was said through the prophet Jeremiah was fulfilled:

18 "A voice was heard in Ramah,
      weeping and great mourning,
   Rachel weeping for her children
      and refusing to be comforted,
   because they were no more."

Joseph settles in Nazareth

Matthew 2:19-23   page 24

19 After Herod died, an angel of the Lord appeared in a dream to Joseph in Egypt **20** and said, "Get up, take the child and his mother and go to the land of Israel, for those who were trying to take the child's life are dead."

21 So he got up, took the child and his mother and went to the land of Israel. **22** But when he heard that Archelaus was reigning in Judea in place of his father Herod, he was afraid to go there. Having been warned in a dream, he withdrew to the district of Galilee, **23** and he went and lived in a town called Nazareth. So was fulfilled what was said through the prophets: "He will be called a Nazarene."

Jesus as a child

Luke 2:41-52   pages 25-27

41 Every year his parents went to Jerusalem for the Feast of the Passover. **42** When he was twelve years old, they went up to the feast, according to the custom. **43** After the feast was over, while his parents were returning home, the boy Jesus stayed behind in Jerusalem, but they were unaware of it. **44** Thinking he was in their company, they travelled on for a day. Then they began looking for him among their relatives and friends. **45** When they did not find him, they went back to Jerusalem to look for him. **46** After three days they found him in the temple courts, sitting among the teachers, listening to them and asking them questions. **47** Everyone who heard him was amazed at his understanding and his answers. **48** When his parents saw him they were astonished. His mother said to him, "Son, why have you treated us like this? Your father and I have been anxiously searching for you."

49 "Why were you searching for me?" he asked. "Didn't you know I had to be in my Father's house?" **50** But they did not understand what he meant.

51 Then he went down to Nazareth with them and was obedient to them. But his mother treasured all these things in her heart. **52** And Jesus grew in wisdom and stature, and in favour with God and men.

Jesus begins his life's work

Matthew 3:13, 4:12-13, Mark 1:15   page 31

13 Then Jesus came from Galilee to the Jordan to be baptized by John.

12 When Jesus heard that John had been put in prison, he returned to Galilee. **13** Leaving Nazareth, he went and lived in Capernaum, which was by the lake in the area of Zebulun and Naphtali.

"The time has come," he said. "The kingdom of God is near. Repent and believe the good news!"

The wedding at Cana

John 2:1-12   pages 28-31

1 On the third day a wedding took place at Cana in Galilee. Jesus' mother was there, **2** and Jesus and his disciples had also been invited to the wedding. **3** When the wine was gone, Jesus' mother said to him, "They have no more wine."

4 "Why do you involve me?" Jesus replied, "My time has not yet come."

5 His mother said to the servants, "Do whatever he tells you."

6 Nearby stood six stone water jars, the kind used by the Jews for ceremonial washing, each holding from seventeen to twenty-five gallons.

7 Jesus said to the servants, "Fill the jars with water"; so they filled them to the brim.

8 Then he told them, "Now draw some out and take it to the master of the banquet."

They did so, **9** and the master of the banquet tasted the water that had been turned into wine. He did not realize where it had come from, though the servants who had drawn the water knew. Then he called the bridegroom aside **10** and said, "Everyone brings out the choice wine first and then the cheaper wine after the guests have had too much to drink; but you have saved the best till now."

11 This, the first of his miraculous signs, Jesus performed in Cana of Galilee. He thus revealed his glory, and his disciples put their faith in him.

12 After this he went down to Capernaum with his mother and brothers and his disciples. Here they stayed for a few days.

Jesus heals the sick

Matthew 4:23   page 31

23 Jesus went throughout Galilee teaching in their synagogues, preaching the good news of the kingdom, and healing every disease and sickness among the people.

People take offence

Luke 4:16-22   pages 32-34

16 He went to Nazareth, where he had been brought up, and on the Sabbath day he went into the synagogue, as was his custom. And he stood up to read. **17** The scroll of the prophet Isaiah was handed to him. Unrolling it, he found the place where it is written:

18 "The Spirit of the Lord is on me;
      therefore he has anointed me to preach
         good news to the poor.
   He has sent me to proclaim freedom
      for the prisoners and recovery of sight
         for the blind,
   to release the oppressed,
19 to proclaim the year of the Lord's favour."

20 Then he rolled up the scroll, gave it back to the attendant and sat down. The eyes of everyone in the synagogue were fastened on him, **21** and he said to them, "Today this scripture is fulfilled in your hearing."

22 All spoke well of him and many who heard him were amazed.

Mark 6:2-3

"Where did this man get these things?" they asked. "What's this wisdom that has been given him, that he even does miracles! 3 Isn't this the carpenter? Isn't this Mary's son and the brother of James, Joses, Judas and Simon? Aren't his sisters here with us?" And they took offence at him.

Jesus' family intervenes

Mark 3:20,21,31-35 pages 35-37

20 Then Jesus entered a house, and again a crowd gathered, so that he and his disciples were not even able to eat. 21 When his family heard about this, they went to take charge of him, for they said, "He is out of his mind."

31 Then Jesus' mother and brothers arrived. Standing outside, they sent someone in to call him. 32 A crowd was sitting around him, and they told him, "Your mother and brothers are outside looking for you."

33 "Who are my mother and my brothers?" he asked.

34 Then he looked at those seated in a circle around him and said, "Here are my mother and my brothers! 35 Whoever does God's will is my brother and sister and mother."

Luke 11:27-28 page 36

27 As Jesus was saying these things, a woman in the crowd called out, "Blessed is the mother who gave you birth and nursed you."

28 He replied, "Blessed rather are those who hear the word of God and obey it."

The opposition gains strength

Luke 4:23-30 pages 37-38

23 Jesus said to them, "Surely you will quote this proverb to me: 'Physician, heal yourself! Do here in your home town what we have heard that you did in Capernaum.' "

24 "I tell you the truth," he continued, "no prophet is accepted in his home town. 25 I assure you that there were many widows in Israel in Elijah's time, when the sky was shut for three and a half years and there was a severe famine throughout the land. 26 Yet Elijah was not sent to any of them, but to a widow in Zarephath in the region of Sidon. 27 And there were many in Israel with leprosy in the time of Elisha the prophet, yet not one of them was cleansed except Naaman the Syrian."

28 All the people in the synagogue were furious when they heard this. 29 They got up, drove him out of the town, and took him to the brow of the hill on which the town was built, in order to throw him down the cliff. 30 But he walked right through the crowd and went on his way.

The crucifixion

John 19:25-27 page 40

25 Near the cross of Jesus stood his mother, his mother's sister, Mary the wife of Clopas, and Mary of Magdala. 26 When Jesus saw his mother there, and the disciple whom he loved standing near by, he said to his mother, "Here is your son," 27 and to the disciple, "Here is your mother." From that time on, this disciple took her into his home.

Mary in the young Church

Acts 1:13-14 page 42

13 When they arrived at Jerusalem, they went upstairs to the room where they were staying. Those present were Peter, John, James and Andrew; Philip and Thomas, Bartholomew and Matthew; James son of Alphaeus and Simon the Zealot, and Judas son of James. 14 They all joined together constantly in prayer, along with the women and Mary the mother of Jesus, and his brothers.

 proost Turnhout (Belgium)